How To Identify Master And Conquer

CHANGE

Uncovering Your Hidden Opportunities

D1713145

Robert Ian

How To Identify
Master And Conquer
CHANGE
Uncovering Your Hidden Opportunities

Robert Ian

Printed in the United States of America.
Cover design by Ad Graphics, Tulsa, OK (800) 368-6196

Library of Congress Control Number: 2002116341
ISBN 0-9725464-0-5

How To Identify, Master And Conquer Change™, *Handbooks For Success*™,
Hypnosis Made Easy™ and *Uncovering Your Hidden Opportunities*™ are
trademarks of Robert Ian Productions, Inc. and Robert Ian, denoting a series
of products that may include but is not limited to books, CDs, DVDs, audio
cassettes and video tapes.

Published by:
Handbooks For Success
a subsidiary of Robert Ian Productions, Inc.
PO Box 250 • New Glarus, WI 53574

Order Information:
To order more copies of this book or other products
by Robert Ian please use the order form
at the back of this book or visit:
www.HandbooksForSuccess.com

Questions, comments or inquiries about booking
Robert Ian to speak in-person at your next meeting,
convention or special event can be emailed to:
publishing@robertian.com

or call toll free:
1-800-800-6194

"Results are always the best credentials"

WHAT PEOPLE ARE SAYING

Here's a sample of what clients and audiences are saying about Robert Ian and his message:

"Robert's message, while certainly entertaining, delivers a 'minds-eye' picture for every day focus. Robert's ability to capture your attention through easy-to-understand concepts has made him my personal 'Head Coach.' Whenever I feel unfocused or unmotivated, I pop in his audiocassette and in no time, I uncover what is missing. My ability to face any problem with a can-do attitude is a result of his teachings. I'm glad his program is now available on CD because I have worn out his tape in my car."

Patrick H. McEvoy, President/CEO
Multi Financial Securities, member ING Advisors Network

* * * * *

"We, at Sysco Food Services of Kansas City, had taken a hiatus from speakers at our annual meetings. Wow, am I glad we chose you to start a 'new era' for us. The message you left with us from 'Expanding the Power of Your Mind' is one we can all use in our career development. We would, without hesitation, recommend you to anyone looking for a uniquely entertaining message on motivation, teamwork and leadership. I want to thank you again for setting a positive tone for the rest of the day. People Magazine was right, you are amazing."

John Jurco, Vice President of Marketing
SYSCO Food Services of Kansas City

* * * * *

"Your focus on preparedness and achieving the impossible really gave our audience something to take away and use in their everyday lives."

Kathleen Wallitsch, Special Events Manager
Blue Cross & Blue Shield of Rhode Island

* * * * *

"In the long history of our association, you are the only speaker we have invited back three times. Your motivational seminar 'The Greatest Secret Never Told' continues to draw positive and enthusiastic comments."

Daniel Ramlow, Executive Director
Kansas Contractors Association, Inc.

"Thank you for a job well done at our National Sales Conference in Vienna, Austria. As your message states 'the key is preparation.' Your presentation was the perfect mix of entertainment, motivation and sound ideas."

Kevin Stych, CFP, VP Sales and Marketing
Locust Street Securities, Inc.

* * * * *

"Robert, I can honestly say that you are one of those extremely rare instances where 'pleased' is too weak a word because we received much more than our money's worth!"

Dick Oehler, Assistant VP of Sales
WACKER Corporation

* * * * *

"The CENTURY 21® system is always looking for the best for the agents that make our company strong and will help them to continue to grow. Your presentation achieved that for us."

Noel Blonquist, Director Performance Development
CENTURY 21® North Central, Inc.

* * * * *

"You allowed our associates to wander into the depths of their minds and find that they have the ability to do amazing things when they apply themselves."

Lawrence Montuori, Director of Associate &
Customer Development, PERDUE FARMS, INC.

* * * * *

"Robert, you are a first-class act."

Lou Holtz, Head Football Coach,
University of South Carolina

* * * * *

"Just a quick note to let you know how much I enjoyed your presentation at last night's MPI meeting. Sometimes motivational speakers present a lot of 'fluff,' but I was really impressed with your content. Thanks for an entertaining, useful and memorable evening."

Sara O'Shea Joshi, Meeting Planner
Michigan Society of Planning Officials

These quotations are excerpted from reference letters on file. They represent a sampling from over 2000 professional appearances worldwide.

OTHER TITLES BY ROBERT IAN

How To Identify Master And Conquer Change
(Book on CD *read by Robert Ian*)

The Greatest Secret Never Told
(90 minute motivational talk on CD)

Stop Smoking
(Self-Hypnosis CD)

Lose Weight
(Self-Hypnosis CD)

Great Golf
(Self-Hypnosis CD)

Sleep Easy
(Self-Hypnosis CD)

Sales Power
(Self-Hypnosis CD)

Success Habits
(Self-Hypnosis CD)

Breaking Mental Barriers
(Self-Hypnosis CD)

Stress-Free Relaxation
(Self-Hypnosis CD)

EZ Public Speaking
(Self-Hypnosis CD)

SPECIAL THANKS

**To some of the individuals who have inspired
me at key points in my life and career:**

Richard Gough
Robert Smith
Alan Stauffacher
Dennis DeYoung
Nathaniel Branden
Joe Charbonneau
Barb Hocker
Bill Menihan
Mary Weisner
Eleanor Woods
Terry Schliem
Knute Hammer
Pam Lontos
Renee Strom
Lynne Rufenacht
Marianne Choquet
Rick Miller
Dennis Connolly
Ed Cantwell
Jim Hennig
Debbie Ferns
Sherbert MacThayer
Skip Wylie
Wayne Dibble

and to my best friend, editor and wife
Sherrill Thayer

Dedicated To The Memory Of

Joe Charbonneau

Who taught me: *If you want to be a master at anything, study the masters who have gone before you, learn to do what they have done, have the guts to do it, and you will be a master just like them.*

Joe passionately believed that you learn from people who have been where you want to go. By studying other people's mistakes and successes, you can shorten your learning curve dramatically.

Look around you right now. Who are the masters that could help shorten your learning curve? These experts are often hidden in plain view. These individuals have the answers you need. You, in turn, may have some of the answers they need. Collaborate. Communicate. Ask questions. Share.

Joe gave me this advice in October of 1987. He was the closing general session speaker for the Wisconsin Grocers Association convention in Milwaukee, Wisconsin. I was the closing luncheon speaker. He was an experienced pro. I was a struggling beginner. We shared a mid-afternoon lunch following my speech. Joe shared a lifetime of wisdom. I listened. He talked. I acted. It worked.

Joe Charbonneau passed away in May of 2001. He touched thousands of lives in his career, including mine. He made a difference.

TABLE OF CONTENTS

"Adults tend to complicate things that should be simple"

Disappearing Balls

Before Jay Leno and David Letterman began hosting late-night television, Johnny Carson was the King of late-night comedy. Johnny, who began his career as an amateur magician (The Great Carsoni), would often invite fellow magicians on *The Tonight Show.*

I recall one night he discussed why adults are easier to fool than children. Johnny said, *"If the magician places a ball in his left hand and the ball disappears, the adult asks 'where did it go?' The kid says 'open the other hand.'"* The kid is right. The magician secretly concealed the ball in his right hand while pretending to place the ball in his left hand.

Magic takes advantage of a person's predictable thinking patterns. Adults tend to think in predictable patterns. When their eyes follow the ball to the left hand and it disappears, they give up. They quit. They say it's impossible. They never realize the answer is just around the corner.

Children, on the other hand, do not think in predictable patterns (yet). When their eyes follow the ball to the left hand and it disappears, they immediately think about where they last saw the ball. *"Aha! It must be in the right hand,"* they say. And usually it is.

Because of their natural curiosity, kids have an uncanny ability to keep their eyes on the ball. Because of their predictable thinking patterns, adults have an uncanny ability to lose track of the ball. Adults tend to complicate things that should be simple.

Most of life's challenges are easy to solve once you look at them realistically. This is because most of the things you worry about never happen. Worry distorts your emotions and clouds your thinking. Worry blinds you to the fact that most of life's challenges are really opportunities in disguise.

Change is one of those challenges. Change creates opportunities that often remain hidden until after the fact. In the meantime, change can result in stress, fear and uncertainty.

If you're like me, you don't want to wait until after the fact. You want to uncover your hidden opportunities right now. It's like eating dessert first. You get a taste of where you're going. You know what it is you're working toward. This allows you to relax and move forward with confidence.

The secret is to let go of predictable thinking patterns and adopt a child-like curiosity about the changes that surround you at this very moment. Curiosity inspires you to ask questions and reach beyond your comfort zone. Some people are afraid to ask questions. They feel asking a question is a sign of weakness. In reality, it's the intelligent people who ask questions. Intelligent people are willing to look like they don't have all the answers in order to get all of the answers they need.

The right question at the right time can help position you for long-term success. I recall a class I took in high school called *The Future*. We talked about science fiction, life in space, genetic engineering and the future impact of technology. The best part was when we talked about designing our own futures.

One day our teacher, Al Stauffacher, said, *"People, how many of you know what you're going to be doing next week?"* I think everyone raised his or her hand.

He said, *"People, how many of you know what you're going to be doing next month?"* About half the hands went up.

He said, *"People, how many of you know what you're going to be doing next year?"* And everyone just looked at each other.

He said, *"People, how many of you know what you're going to be doing five years from now?"* The room was silent.

He said, *"People, how many of you know what you're going to be doing ten or fifteen years from now?* You could have heard a pin drop.

Then he paused for the longest time and said, *"People, that's the problem. Most of us don't have a clear picture of where we're going in life. You can't know exactly what you'll be doing fifteen years from now, but everything you're doing today is going to shape those next fifteen years and more. Open your eyes to the opportunities that surround you right now. Ask questions. Be daring. Be creative. Take a chance. Fifteen years from now, you'll be glad you did."*

That message is just as relevant today whether you are eighteen, thirty-three, forty-eight or sixty-three years old. It doesn't matter what you have or haven't done up until this point, *it's from now on that counts.*

Today is the first day of the rest of your life.

Are you ready for a performance breakthrough?
It's possible...and easier than you think.

Let's go back to the disappearing ball trick. On the surface, it appears to be impossible. On closer examination, the solution is quite simple.

Change is much the same way. On the surface, it can appear to be impossible. On closer examination, the solution is often quite simple. When you look even closer, you will uncover the hidden opportunities that surround you at this very moment.

The title of this book explains the process: *How To Identify, Master And Conquer Change.*

You identify change by asking the right questions of yourself and those around you. Questions you would normally "push aside" for another day. Questions that cause you to think. Questions that demand more than a simple yes or no answer. Questions that make you uncomfortable. Questions that challenge *your* status quo. Questions that ask you to examine your needs, wants and desires. Questions that inspire you to reach beyond your comfort zone. Questions that require you to expand the power of your mind.

You master change by *realistically* assessing the resources and options available to you at this very moment. Realistic means being honest with yourself. Decisions based on honest analysis keep you grounded in reality and help position you for long-term success.

Achieving that success means understanding the difference between instant and delayed gratification. Some kinds of change produce instant gratification. The benefits are immediately known. Other kinds of change produce delayed gratification. The benefits are not realized until later. In a world of instant coffee, instant email and instant oil changes, delayed gratification is a tough sell. That's why change itself can be a tough sell.

When things get difficult, uncomfortable or hard to manage, *that's the time* to start probing deeper and uncovering your hidden opportunities.

In my experience, both personally and professionally, the most effective technique for managing change is the sentence completion exercise. Dr. Nathaniel Branden, author of *The Six Pillars of Self Esteem* and *Honoring The Self,* pioneered this technique. It allows you to access vital information you already possess which lies beyond your conscious awareness.

Do this: Rapidly write six endings for the following incomplete sentence (called a sentence stem). Do not censor your thoughts. If you get stuck, repeat or invent an ending. The endings you write do not have to be literally true. Just write whatever comes to mind. Move swiftly. Make each ending grammatically correct. See how ideas hidden inside you begin rising to the surface. Here's an example:

If I approach change as an opportunity...

- ***It won't scare me as much***
- ***I'll look for the positives***
- ***I know I can make it work for me***
- ***There will be a lot to learn***
- ***Success is just around the corner***
- ***I'll find something to like about it***

Now it's your turn. Write six endings for this sentence stem:

If I approach change as an opportunity...

_____

_____

_____

_____

_____

_____

You conquer change by *doing* something about it.

Action changes everything.

Let's get started.

"You get what you expect"

Do you expect the best?

YOUR MAGIC MIND

You are standing on the shore of the greatest uncharted territory of all time. This is a magical place where ideas are more valuable than gold, platinum or diamonds. This is a place where the motor that drives the world is fueled, not by physical energy, but rather, by mental energy. You have entered the realm of your own mind.

Throughout history, the human mind has been our only means of survival. In a physical contest between the strongest human being and a lion, alligator or other ferocious beast, the beast would surely win. Throughout history human beings have survived, not because of their physical strength, but rather, because of their mental strength.

Your mind is a powerful force. It is your greatest asset. The results you produce in today's fast-changing world are directly related to how well you use your mind.

In many ways, your mind is like a magic mirror. It reflects back to you exactly what you place in front of it. Negative thoughts create negative results. Positive thoughts create positive results. Remember the old saying, *"be careful what you wish for, you just might get it?"* There's a lot of truth in that statement. This is because your mind operates on the principle of self-fulfilling prophecy. Six magic words describe the process: You become what you think about.

You think about driving to work and sure enough, you're there before you know it. You think about getting married and sure enough, you meet someone and fall in love. You think about buying a new computer and sure enough, you're at the keyboard in no time flat. The process works every time.

This process is extremely important when it comes to making the most out of change. This is because *you get what you expect.* Do you expect the best?

- Do you expect you will discover hidden opportunities?
- Do you expect you will rise above difficult challenges?
- Do you expect you will out-think your competition?
- Do you expect you will solve problems successfully?
- Do you expect you will participate on a winning team?
- Do you expect you will be happy and enjoy yourself?
- Do you expect you will learn and grow?
- Do you expect your future will be bright?

Managing change is about managing expectations. Expect the best and you will get the best.

Perhaps you have been asked the age-old question *"is the glass half-full or half-empty?"*

Half empty signifies you are a pessimist, a negative thinker. You are someone who looks at life and expects nothing more than mediocrity.

Half full signifies you are an optimist, a positive thinker. You are someone who looks at life and expects the best.

Change can be viewed in much the same way. How do you look at change?

Do you look at change as a predator? An enemy who stalks you every waking moment? Do you see it as a process that robs you of stability, consistency and peace of mind?

Or do you look at change as a friend? A companion who escorts you on this fascinating journey called life? Do you see it as a process that creates opportunities and inspires you to raise the bar on your own performance?

Change can be all of these things or some of these things. This is because you define the meaning of change by your choices and actions.

You get what you expect. Expect the best.

"Most of the things you worry about never happen"

CHANGE IS GOOD: YOU TRY IT FIRST

I recall a breakfast cereal commercial on television. Two brothers were arguing over who was going to be the first to try a new brand of cereal. Then the solution dawned on them. They would get their younger brother to try the cereal. They figured he wouldn't eat it because he hates everything. Much to their surprise, their younger brother liked the cereal and quickly finished his bowl. The older brothers filled their bowls and were seen enjoying the cereal as the commercial ended.

The prospect of change worried the older brothers. They were afraid the new cereal would taste terrible. They believed if it was such a good idea, then someone else should try it first. Starting at a young age, most people begin to worry about change. Their imagination becomes their worst enemy.

Think about all the stress-producing, anxiety-filled changes you have experienced in your life. Think about how upset you were at the time. Think about the arguments, the fear and the uncertainty. Think about the tremendous amount of energy you invested because you were worried about the outcome.

Now ask yourself: *"How much energy have I wasted over the years worrying about things that never happened?"*

If you answered *"a lot"* or *"more than I would have cared to,"* then your imagination has been a serious enemy. The good news is you can do something about it right now. Your imagination can become your best friend. From now on, you can relax and move forward with confidence. You can actually enjoy the process of change. Just remember this one simple idea: *Most of the things you worry about never happen.*

Worry, left unchecked, can cloud your thinking and lead to the development of imaginary limitations. Imaginary limitations are created in the mind and have no basis in reality. These limitations can:

- Make you afraid to try something new
- Prevent you from accomplishing your goals
- Cause you to give up before you ever start

Almost all of the limitations you face will be imaginary. Their origin will be fear in one form or another:

- Fear of success
- Fear of failure
- Fear of being uncomfortable
- Fear of accepting responsibility
- Fear of admitting a truth you have tried to deny
- Fear of the unknown
- Fear of being happy
- Fear of change

When you believe in limitations that are imaginary, it's like setting negative goals. You get what you don't want.

Another symptom of imaginary limitations is the *"it could be worse"* syndrome. To rationalize less than desirable outcomes, people often say:

- It could be worse, I might have come in *last*
- It could be worse, I might have lost *all* my money
- It could be worse, I might have broken *both* legs

The problem with this mindset is that we're always comparing ourselves with the worst, not the best. Yes, it's true, things can always be worse. That's not the point. The possibility of things being worse is not grounds to accept a situation you would like to change.

When you think about problems realistically, you begin to put them in perspective. New foods, even if you don't care for them, *rarely taste terrible*. Most problems are *not catastrophic*. Most changes *do not hurt*. Things may be uncomfortable for a while, but they are *seldom awful*.

Think about the real and anticipated changes you are facing. Think about any fear or anxiety you may be experiencing. With those thoughts in mind, write six endings for this sentence stem:

If I look at my current situation realistically...

_____

_____

_____

_____

_____

_____

When you look at change realistically, you will empower yourself to uncover hidden opportunities. You will find imaginary limitations begin to fade away like a desert mirage.

Then perhaps you'll say: *"Change is good, I'll try it first."*

"Winners are losers who got up and gave it just one more try"

— *Dennis DeYoung*

THE IMPOSSIBLE IS ACHIEVABLE

Ever since I was a young boy, I have always wanted to know how the world worked. When I was eight years old, I had a laboratory in our basement at home. After school, I would conduct scientific experiments using my junior chemistry set. My parents were glad I never blew the house up and were happier when I was ten years old and got interested in magic. A curious son couldn't do too much damage with a deck of cards.

I soon discovered that one of the country's best magic instructors lived in Rockford, IL, about an hour from my hometown of Monroe, WI. I had to meet him. His name was Richard Gough. My parents took turns driving me to Rockford so I could take Saturday morning magic classes. This went on for years. I learned everything from card tricks to rope tricks to mind reading illusions.

Magic teaches more than just tricks. It reveals a unique psychology for solving problems. When you witness a mind-boggling illusion, you immediately try to reconstruct how it was accomplished. As you backtrack, your mind's ability to make logical connections breaks down. This puts your mind into a "feedback loop" and creates the illusion of magic.

People are supposed to look at magic and say, "that's impossible." Unfortunately, people often look at success in all of its various forms and say, "*that's* impossible". These areas of success vary from one profession to another but often include:

- Making more sales
- Managing people better
- Providing better customer service
- Creating and sustaining effective relationships
- Improving safety performance
- Learning how to use new technology
- Increasing productivity and performance

In all of these cases, if you look just below the surface, you'll find there is a strategy you can use to achieve the desired results. *By learning to solve the "impossible," you can achieve the "impossible."*

Achieving the "impossible" requires persistence. Small children achieve the impossible everyday. Children learn at an incredible rate of speed. A rate of speed they will most likely never again achieve. Children try everything. They do not worry about looking foolish. During this phenomenal learning curve children experience many failures, upsets and defeats and rarely give them a second thought. A child's ability to learn illustrates the fact that *winners are losers who got up and gave it just one more try.*

It's only as we grow into adolescence and adulthood that our ability to learn slows down and sometimes stagnates. Parents and teachers instill fear. Children are punished for failure or not providing the "correct" or "right" answers. Peer pressure influences kids to conform to the crowd. Individualism is slowly sacrificed. As adults the process continues. We're led to believe the answer is more government, more regulation and more conformity. As a result, the fear of failure is overwhelming. People become afraid to try anything new. They would never permit themselves to think of doing something even slightly radical or innovative. If their neighbors aren't doing it, and their colleagues at work aren't doing it, and their family isn't doing it, and the people in their social circle aren't doing it, then they are not going to do it. It's sad but true, but by the time we're in our 30's and 40's, most of us have a long list of things we will never try again because we tried them once and failed.

Behold the turtle! He only gets somewhere when he sticks his neck out! You can only get somewhere when you venture outside of your comfort zone. The first thing you must do is adopt the mindset of a creative person. The creative person expects to win. Expects to create ideas. Expects to solve problems. The creative person knows that the difference between successful and unsuccessful people is that successful people have *formed the habits* of doing those things unsuccessful people dislike doing and will not do.

The question is: *"can everyone think creatively?"* Or *"is creative thinking a luxury reserved for the gifted few?"* The good news is, yes, everyone can think creatively and, no, creative thinking is not a luxury reserved for the gifted few.

Why then are there apparently so few creative thinkers? Why aren't more people actively creative? The answer is disarmingly simple. Most people have an intense fear of being wrong. They have an intense fear of being laughed at or not accepted. As a result, they stifle their own creativity. They rely on other people to be the "creative ones." By adopting this mindset, people perform a monstrous injustice to themselves. They deny themselves the joy that results from an adrenalin high; a mental high that comes when you figure out a new idea or solve a problem. It's a feeling of pride, self-confidence, self-esteem and a feeling of power in your mind's ability to think.

When you experience this mental high your pulse quickens, your muscles tense, there's a high level of internal excitement. Life suddenly becomes perfect. You have a feeling of momentary immortality. This incredible feeling of internal self-worth is the reward of creative thinking. It doesn't matter if the idea you create is small or the problem you solve is large. The feeling is the same. It doesn't matter how valuable or earth-shattering the idea is. The important thing is that you created it.

There is a vast, untapped, unlimited resource of creative ideas within each of us. Michelangelo once said, *"The idea is there, locked inside. All you have to do is remove the excess stone."* Your ability to identify, master and conquer change begins when you start to remove *your* excess stone. An idea is the most valuable commodity there is. Ideas are the required currency for uncovering your hidden opportunities. Never underestimate the potential power of your ideas.

- If Christopher Columbus hadn't dared to follow-through on his idea to sail west, where would we be today?

- If Ben Franklin hadn't dared to go fly a kite, where would we be today?

- If Alexander Graham Bell hadn't dared to follow-through on his idea to transmit sound over wires, where would we be today?

- If Thomas Edison hadn't dared to follow-through on his ideas to record sound, record pictures with a film camera and use electricity to transform a filament wire into light, where would we be today?

- If Henry Ford hadn't dared to follow-through on his idea to use an assembly line to mass-produce automobiles, where would we be today?

- If Steve Jobs, Steve Wozniak and Bill Gates hadn't dared to follow-through on their ideas for creating personal computers and the software to run them, where would we be today?

If you fail to think creatively and follow-through on your ideas, no matter how large or small they may be; where will you, your family and your organization be tomorrow, next week or next year?

The choice and responsibility are up to you.

"A goal is a dream with a deadline"

BUILD CHANGE INTO YOUR GOALS

When organizations invite me to speak at their events, I will often present a version of my *Hypnosis Show and Motivational Talk*™. As an introduction to this program, I sometimes perform the following illusion:

A one hundred dollar bill is borrowed from an audience member. The bill is autographed by its owner for later identification. In exchange for the bill, the participant is given a brown paper bag. The bill is set on fire and burned to ashes. The participant opens the bag and finds a large grapefruit. The grapefruit is cut open to reveal a soggy green piece of paper. The participant unfolds the green piece of paper and discovers it is the fully restored and autographed one hundred dollar bill.

This illusion illustrates an important point. A large grapefruit is approximately the same size as the average human brain as it sits inside your skull. Inside your brain there are literally hundreds and hundreds of hundred dollar bills with *your* name on them, waiting to get out and find their way into your pocket, your bank account and your lifestyle. These bills can take the form of money, ideas or new skills.

But what's the secret? How do you get these hundred dollar bills out of your brain and into your pocket?

The real secret is that *there is no secret* because great minds have been telling us the real secret for generations. The secret is a universal story. Every time I think about this story I think about the caption to a cartoon I once saw:

Customer in antique shop: *"What's new?"*

The idea behind this cartoon caption is that *what's new is old*. The secret I'm referring to is age old, but it's packaging is new. Take a look at the business and self-help section of any bookstore. When you boil down and add up the contents of most of these books, you often get the same story. The names change and the faces change, but the story is often the same.

- Perhaps it's a high school athlete who champions him or herself to become an Olympic superstar.

- Perhaps it's someone who starts a business in his or her basement with a few thousand dollars and turns it into a multi-million dollar enterprise.

- Perhaps it's one of the millions of people who set goals every day and then sets out to achieve them.

It's a universal story with five key points. I refer to them as:

The Universal Laws for Mastering Change

1. **Believe in yourself.** You must believe in your ability to accomplish the change you desire. If you don't believe in yourself, then it's going to be difficult for other people to believe in you.

2. **Define your goals.** You must know *specifically* the kind of change you want if you're ever going to create it. You must set short, medium and long-term goals. Do this on a regular basis with a timetable for accomplishment. A goal is a dream with a deadline.

3. **Define your plan.** You must have a written plan or blueprint explaining how you will proceed. You must break down each goal into a series of smaller goals that can be accomplished one step at a time. This creates a roadmap for change.

4. **Be willing to work.** You must make a conscious choice to give your goals the necessary time, effort and energy to make them happen.

5. **Do it.** You must take action. Take your best shot and go for it. If you fail, do not give up. Re-think your plan and try it again and again until you create the kind of change you desire. Remember, *winners are losers who got up and gave it just one more try.*

You'll find that you are working to accomplish a variety of goals all at the same time. When you achieve one goal, set out to achieve another. You'll find that you occasionally modify or even abandon one goal in lieu of another. This is the nature of change. It's important to *build change into your goals.*

Write it down. Be specific. It's much easier to aim at, and hit, a target you can clearly see. Words are like a lens that can help focus your mind. The more specific your goals, the more likely you are to achieve them.

Early in my career, I was the keynote speaker at an automotive convention. I had just explained the importance of writing down goals and being specific. Halfway through the presentation, a gentleman in the audience raised his hand and shared the results of his personal experience.

He explained that about eight years before, he had taken a class on goal setting. One of the assignments was to create a journal of what his life would look like ten years in the future. He wrote down the kind of home he would live in. Where it would be located. How many children he and his wife would have. He wrote down accomplishments he would make in his career. He described vacations he and his family would take. He wrote down how he would structure his retirement plan. He discussed his private pilot's license.

He told the audience that he had packed the journal away and forgotten about it. That is, until he and his wife moved into their new home last year. He found the journal and read it from cover to cover. Much to his amazement, *he had achieved every goal he had written down in that journal.* Everything, that is, except obtaining his private pilot's license. He assured the audience he would be doing that over the next year.

This is a clear example of how your mind operates on the principle of self-fulfilling prophecy. When you write down goals that are serious and specific, you enter into an unspoken contract with yourself. This sets your mind into motion making connections to help you achieve your goals.

Here's an example of how people sometimes look at goals:

When I am clear about my goals…

- *They are much easier to achieve*
- *Change doesn't scare me as much*
- *I feel they are within reach*
- *I am in control*
- *I feel relaxed*
- *Life is fulfilling*

Now it's your turn. Write six endings for this sentence stem:

One of the goals I need to be clear about...

_____

_____

_____

_____

_____

_____

Select one of the goals you have just written and describe it in as much detail as you can.

- Don't just write *"a lot of money"* – put a specific dollar amount on it.

- Don't just write *"a nice home"* – describe in detail each room.

- Don't just write *"a more challenging job"* – describe in detail your increased responsibilities.

- Don't just write *"a happy family life"* – describe in detail your relationship with your spouse, your children, and the activities you would engage in.

The goal I need to be clear about is:

_____

Describe this goal in detail:

_____

_____

_____

_____

Now, write six endings for this sentence stem:

To achieve this goal I need to…

_____

_____

_____

_____

_____

_____

Repeat this process for the other five goals you identified on the previous page.

"It is not necessary to change. Survival is not mandatory."

– W. Edwards Deming

ORGANIZATIONAL CHANGE

Throughout the course of my career, I have spoken to over 2000 organizations across North America including corporations, trade associations, government agencies, educational institutions and small businesses.

To help prepare myself for each speaking engagement, I ask my clients to complete a pre-program questionnaire. The purpose of this questionnaire is to discuss the changes that have impacted that client's organization over the previous twelve months. The details of these questionnaires are confidential. However, there are a number of common and universal themes I can share. These themes account for over 80% of all organizational change and will continue to form the basis of organizational change well into the next decade.

Overlapping circles. Organizational change is best viewed as a series of overlapping circles. Each circle represents the changes taking place in different organizations. The parts that overlap represent either common or universal changes.

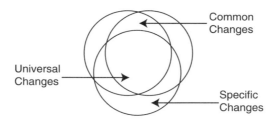

Universal changes affect all organizations. Common changes affect most organizations. Specific changes affect one organization. While it is true that all organizations are faced with specific changes, these are often tied to common or universal changes.

The following items are widely reported areas of common and universal organizational change (in no particular order):

- Grew too fast
- Mergers (buying out your competitor)
- Industry partnerships
- Environmental regulations
- Government regulations
- Lots of new employees
- Increasing competition
- Consolidation
- Deregulation
- Implementation of random drug testing program
- Low unemployment (need for employees)
- Loss of key people due to illness or retirement
- Need to attract new committee chairs and volunteer leaders
- Over-production
- Lower prices (deflation)
- Each year more competitors going out of business
- Servicing new equipment in the field
- Absorbing new responsibilities
- Downsizing
- Outsourcing
- Doing more with less
- Job retention
- Reimbursement pressure
- Demographic changes

- Employee retention
- Rapid technological change
- Steep learning curve
- Marginal service (due to fast growth)
- Recession's negative impact on commissions and morale
- Excess inventory
- Rising prices
- Unpredictable climate changes
- Health insurance premiums
- Bad press (our industry is in the gutter along with stock market)
- September 11th downfall in economy and sales
- Resistance to technology – people asking: *"how is this going to make my life easier?"*
- Business relationships at a premium (due to consolidation of customers)

Eight out of ten readers will find the major changes affecting their organizations in the preceding list. If you have not identified the changes relevant to your organization, please write six endings for this sentence stem:

One of the changes I must now face...

_____

_____

_____

_____

_____

_____

Once you become clear about the changes you must face, new questions can surface in the back of your mind. These can include:

- Am I being pulled in too many directions?
- How many choices and options do I really have?
- How can I partner with others to solve problems?
- What kind of timeframe am I working with?
- What if I don't know how to proceed?
- What if the unpredictable occurs?
- Are there any other reasonable alternatives?
- Where can I turn for guidance and inspiration?
- How can I provide leadership?
- What if I fail?

These questions can be overwhelming when you are in the middle of an important change. This is a critical time. It's easy to get sidetracked and lose your focus. This is the moment when you must look through the clear lens of reality.

Here's what some people see when they look through that clear lens:

If I look at my situation realistically...

- *I am not afraid anymore*
- *There are lots of options*
- *I can actually have fun with this*
- *I am going to succeed*
- *It makes me wonder why I've been so worked up*
- *My mind relaxes*

The key word in the previous sentence stem is "realistically." When you look at something realistically, it compels you to be honest. Fear, anxiety and imaginary limitations are checked at the door. Suddenly, you have a clear perspective. You feel you are back in control of your situation. And you know what? You are.

Now it's your turn. Think about your current situation. Think about everything that frustrates you about this situation. Now write six endings for this sentence stem:

If I look at my situation realistically...

_____

_____

_____

_____

_____

_____

Once you have identified the changes that surround you and realistically examined their potential impact, the next step is to take some kind of action. Action steps are as unique as the individuals who create them. Your action steps will be a direct reflection of the specific changes you are facing right now.

To help stimulate your thinking, here are some of the action steps and ideas my clients most often want to instill in their audiences as a result of listening to one of my live speeches:

- Everyone is a leader
- Not all change is bad
- Create quality products
- Build quality relationships
- Get ahead of schedule and under budget
- Everyone has different barriers – break yours
- Enjoy life – stop and smell the roses
- Develop a new perspective
- Barriers to personal and professional success are just an illusion
- A new beginning is as simple as a change of attitude
- Step forward and share your areas of expertise
- Take calculated risks
- Become involved
- Try new ideas
- Safety is the number one concern
- Find and implement best practices
- Think outside the box
- Realize the many tools you have available
- Sales reps should be thinking about our product on every sales call
- Economy has not created panic – we're in this for the long haul
- There is an opportunity for success even when you're faced with greater competition
- Our primary concern is our customers and what is best for them
- Maximize sales growth with supplier partnership
- Even in a changing business there is a future – it just may be a little different

- Sell more and have fun doing it
- Balance between work and family
- Reduce stress – use relaxation techniques
- If we don't change our vision we are in jeopardy
- What you do impacts others
- Relationships are the most important part of our job
- Are you enjoying life to the fullest? If not, start making changes today
- If we are not moving forward, the competition is passing us
- Success starts with a vision of where you want to go

Now it's your turn. Think about the changes you have identified and how you can look at them realistically. Read over the information you have written down. Now that your mind is swimming in ideas, write as many endings as you can for this sentence stem:

If any of what I have written is true, it might be helpful if I…

_____

_____

_____

_____

_____

Pick one of the endings you have just written (the one you believe is most important) and place an asterisk* next to it. Read that sentence over and over again. Really think about. Internalize what it means. Now write as many endings as you can for this sentence stem:

To accomplish this I need to...

_____

_____

_____

_____

_____

_____

Action changes everything. You can start right now by picking one of the action steps you just created and DO IT. Nothing happens until you take action. Repeat the process described in this chapter for each area of organizational change you must navigate.

Change, just like success, is a moving target. As you implement the action steps you have created there are a number of important factors to keep in mind:

The Unknown: People are naturally cautious about the unknown. No one wants to make a mistake. Keep this in mind as you learn new skills and adopt new ways of doing things. Be sensitive to other people in their time of change.

Feeling Defensive: Change can sometimes be viewed as a threat instead of an opportunity in disguise. The key to minimizing defensive feelings in yourself and others is clear communication.

Morale and Motivation: If you are unable to deliver on anticipated changes, tell those individuals who will be affected in a positive way. Explain the reasons why things will not proceed as planned and outline the next step. Keeping people "in the loop" helps maintain morale and motivation.

Disagreements: People in different parts of an organization often view change differently. Genuine disagreements can result. Before you leave an angry voicemail or send an abrupt email, take a break and consider what you are about to say. It's okay to disagree but it's best to couple your disagreement with a specific suggestion for doing things better.

Organizational change is not a new trend. It is a process that is here to stay. Recognizing this process as part of everyday life will position you for long-term success. You can minimize the negative impact of changes outside of your control by remaining tenacious and committed. This attitude will keep you focused on the changes you can control and help you uncover the hidden opportunities that surround you at this very moment.

"*It is not the strongest of the species that survive, nor the most intelligent, but the one most responsive to change*"

– Charles Darwin

PERSONAL CHANGE

The Chinese symbol for "crisis" contains two elements that represent "danger" and "opportunity." Regardless of your situation, no matter how great the perceived danger, at the heart of every crisis lies a tremendous opportunity.

The road to personal change requires you to look at who you are, where you've been and where you want to go. The process is similar to that of organizational change, but the kind of information you examine will be much more personal and potentially more uncomfortable.

Being uncomfortable is okay. It prompts you to consider ideas that would otherwise remain unspoken. This process can lead to resistance. Resistance is that great unseen power that persuades you to choose safety and comfort over growth and challenge.

Personal change is all about growth and challenge. Think about how you would answer the following questions:

- At this point in your life, what do you really want?
- What would you like to change about your life?
- What are your biggest fears about these changes?
- Is there anything missing in your life?

- Do you have the necessary support system to help you create the changes you desire?
- Who is supportive of your desire for change?
- Who is not supportive of your desire for change?
- Are you willing to reach out and ask for help from those who are supportive?
- What steps have you taken to create the changes you desire?
- Do you feel there are any internal roadblocks to your success?
- Do you have any specific goals?
- If so, what are they?
- What is your timeframe for accomplishing these goals?
- Are you ready to take action?
- Are you prepared for any failure or discomfort you may experience?
- Are you ready to seize the hidden opportunities you will uncover along the way?
- How do you see yourself five years from now?

You can gain confidence in your ability to change by starting out with low-risk changes. Visit a new restaurant. Pick up a magazine you've never read before. Try something new on the menu. Type a subject you don't know anything about into your favorite search engine and see where it takes you. Take a weekend trip and visit a new place. Invite your neighbors over for dinner. Start a new hobby. Small victories add up to increased confidence.

When you're ready for something more daring, begin by thinking back to an important change in your life. What was it? How did you feel at the time? What were your fears? How did you overcome them? By examining your own previous situations, you can uncover strategies for change that have already proven successful. You can recycle these strategies and apply them to the changes you now face.

The time lag between a major change and the appearance of any visible benefits can cause stress, fear and uncertainty. Minor problems can become magnified and intensified. Important decisions made in an emotional moment can be reckless. This can lead to the development of new problems and more stress. If you begin to feel overly stressed:

- Take a nap
- Take a walk
- Take a day off
- Take a vacation
- Learn to say no
- Learn how to relax (self-hypnosis)
- Talk out your problems
- Eat healthier (avoid junk food, sugar and caffeine)

These activities can help minimize the situational stress that results from dealing with personal change. Keep in mind that some stress is beneficial. Driving on an icy road is stressful but it keeps you alert. Giving a speech can be stressful but it keeps you focused on doing a good job. There are, however, a number of things that may signal you are under too much stress. For example:

- The quality of your work is starting to diminish
- You complain more and are easily irritated
- You eat more and exercise less
- You sleep more and have less energy
- You give less attention to your appearance

If these kinds of symptoms persist over time and begin to significantly affect the quality of your life, it would be wise to consult your healthcare provider for further evaluation.

A common theme that has emerged from interviews with my clients and audience members is that change does create opportunities. Unfortunately, these opportunities often remain hidden until after the fact. In other words, when you are in the middle of a major life change it's hard to see any future benefits. When viewed in retrospect months or years later, the benefits are obvious. This applies to changes you initiate yourself as well as those that are thrust upon you. ***It's always easier to look back at things that have already happened than it is to look forward and imagine that you are looking back at where you are right now.***

Pretend for a moment that this book is a time machine. As you hold these pages and read these words you begin to move forward in history. You arrive fifteen years into the future. You realize you have finally become the person you have always wanted to be. But something is troubling you. In the back of your mind there's a little voice that keeps saying you could have arrived here a whole lot sooner. To solve this nagging mystery you think back to the changes you were facing fifteen years ago (today) and realize that most of things you worried about never happened. In fact, there were opportunities all around you at that time, but you didn't see them as such. You allowed fear and stress to blind you to something that was hidden in plain view. You wish now that you could go back in time and take advantage of those opportunities because you are certain you would have arrived at this place much sooner. Hold on, something's happening! This time machine is moving back in history precisely fifteen years. You have returned to the here and now. There's just one difference. You can see the opportunities that surround you at this very moment. The amazing thing is that you could not see them a moment ago. With these thoughts in mind, write six endings for this sentence stem:

One of the opportunities that's coming into focus...

_____

_____

_____

_____

_____

_____

Place an asterisk* next to the ending you believe is most important. Now write six endings for this sentence stem:

To get the most out of this opportunity...

_____

_____

_____

_____

_____

_____

Change *begins to work for you* instead of against you when you start to uncover your hidden opportunities.

"*The important thing is not to stop questioning*"

— Albert Einstein

THE GREATEST SECRET NEVER TOLD

The greatest secret never told is simply this: I believe *there isn't a problem or a challenge that you face in your life right now for which you do not already know the answer.*

You may not like some of the answers you uncover. These answers may involve stepping outside your comfort zone. But you can discover these answers. Once you do, there are only two choices available:

1. Accept the current situation.
2. Take action to change the situation.

In each case, you are fully aware of your choice. You accept responsibility for your action or inaction. The third option of "default" disappears.

Default is what happens when you never ask yourself tough, probing questions. You allow yourself to "zone out" and drift into the mental fog of avoidance and denial. Default is what I call the game of "mind reading."

Mind reading is great form of entertainment. It is a disastrous method of communication. Whether you are trying to "read" your own mind or the minds of others, the results are the same: miscommunication and missed opportunities.

How many times have you been disappointed because you expected someone else to respond to a question that was never asked in the first place? You thought to yourself:

- He *knows* what I mean
- She *knows* what I mean
- They *know* what I mean

Or worse yet, you fooled yourself into thinking:

- I *know* what I mean (without being clear to yourself)

No one knows what you mean (including yourself) unless you clearly say what you mean. I shudder when I think about how many relationships have been ruined, how many sales have been lost and how many lives have been turned upside-down because of this destructive game called mind reading.

Throughout this book, you have performed several sentence completion exercises. In the coming pages, I want you to rapidly write six grammatically correct endings for each of the following sentence stems. Do not censor your thoughts. Don't worry if each ending is literally true. The important thing is to keep writing. If you get stuck, invent an ending or repeat a previous one. See how answers you thought you didn't have begin to bubble up to surface.

If I approach my learning curve with confidence...

_____

_____

_____

_____

_____

_____

If I don't take setbacks as personal defeats...

_____

_____

_____

_____

_____

The hard thing about managing change...

_____

_____

_____

_____

_____

_____

One of the changes I must soon face...

_____

_____

_____

_____

_____

_____

If I look at these changes realistically...

_____

_____

_____

_____

_____

If I embrace change as an opportunity...

_____

_____

_____

_____

_____

_____

One of the things I've had a hard time coping with...

_____

_____

_____

_____

_____

_____

Teamwork flourishes when...

_____

_____

_____

_____

_____

To increase my value at work…

_____

_____

_____

_____

_____

_____

Five years from now…

_____

_____

_____

_____

_____

To become even more successful…

_____

_____

_____

_____

_____

_____

If you could read my mind…

_____

_____

_____

_____

_____

_____

When I take my personal relationships seriously…

_____

_____

_____

_____

_____

_____

I am happiest when…

_____

_____

_____

_____

_____

_____

If I were more aware of my customer's needs…

_____

_____

_____

_____

_____

If my attitude were contagious…

_____

_____

_____

_____

_____

_____

I have fun with stressful situations when I...

_____

_____

_____

_____

_____

_____

When I go out of my way to cheer other people on...

_____

_____

_____

_____

_____

_____

When I give people my full attention...

_____

_____

_____

_____

_____

_____

One of the things I don't know how to ask for...

_____

_____

_____

_____

_____

_____

At this point in my life...

_____

_____

_____

_____

_____

_____

A good way to stabilize our work environment...

_____

_____

_____

_____

_____

_____

When I raise the bar on my own performance...

_____

_____

_____

_____

_____

_____

When I view change from someone else's perspective...

_____

_____

_____

_____

_____

_____

If learning is a lifelong experience...

_____

_____

_____

_____

_____

To bring out the best in other people...

_____

_____

_____

_____

_____

_____

When I sense someone feels threatened or anxious...

_____

_____

_____

_____

_____

If a goal I perceive as impossible really is achievable...

_____

_____

_____

_____

_____

_____

You have just identified a tremendous amount of information about yourself. Take some time and look over everything you have written. Look for any patterns that may be emerging. Now finish these action-oriented sentence completions:

If any of what I have just written is true, then it might be helpful if I…

_____

_____

_____

_____

_____

_____

As I prepare to write the next chapter of my professional life, it might be helpful if I…

_____

_____

_____

_____

_____

_____

As I prepare to write the next chapter of my personal life, it might be helpful if I…

_____

_____

_____

_____

_____

_____

"All I will ever be exists within me now. If I am to be what my dreams expect of me, then I must reach into my soul and tear down those intimidating walls of fear that have so many times stopped me before."

— Mark MacInnis

Permission To Succeed

When you were a child you asked your parents, teachers, brothers and sisters for permission to do things. Now, as an adult, you don't need to ask permission. You're free to think for yourself and make your own choices.

However, at some level, you may still be waiting for some*one* to give you permission to be more successful than you are now.

- Permission to be happy
- Permission to make more sales
- Permission to make a grumpy person smile
- Permission to be more successful than your parents
- Permission to wake up to the possibilities of life
- Permission to be who you really are
- Permission to fall in love
- Permission to change
- Permission to succeed

Perhaps right now you're waiting for permission to make a major breakthrough. Waiting for someone you care about or respect to read your mind and say it's okay.

You think if you wait long enough, someday it will just happen. For most people, that someday never comes.

The solution? From now on: *Give yourself permission to succeed.* Say to yourself: *"Permission granted."*

Complacency can kill you. People joke you should never let the truth get in the way of a good story. This is one of those instances. It's the story about an alleged scientific experiment of how a frog deals with change.

In the experiment, a scientist placed a frog into a bowl of boiling water. The frog jumped out of the water with lightning-fast reflexes. The frog would not tolerate a change from room temperature to 212 degrees boiling. Every time the frog was placed in the water, it jumped out with similar speed. Other frogs were placed in the water and they too, jumped out immediately.

After establishing the fact that no frog would tolerate a change of this kind, the scientist placed a frog in a bowl of water at room temperature. A Bunsen burner, which is a gas-operated candle, was placed under the bowl of water. Over a period of several hours, the water temperature slowly increased. The temperature change was so gradual the frog did not really notice it. The frog accepted each incremental change until a bubble rose to the surface of the water. Then there was another bubble and instantly the entire bowl of water was boiling to the top. The frog boiled to death. It died of its own complacency.

Why did the frog die? Because it chose to ignore the changes that were taking place around it. The frog pretended that if it did not acknowledge change, then change would not affect it. The frog proved that it is possible to ignore the warning signs of an impending disaster, but only temporarily.

When complacency strikes, it's easy to ignore change. This can only continue for a while. Crisis management should be the exception, not the rule. Change is often resisted until it affects you directly and financially. It's only when you wake up one morning and discover you have no money in your wallet and only change in your pocket that you realize now is the time to identify, master and conquer change – before it conquers you.

In the early 1980's, I began my career as a professional magician entertaining every weekend at the former Lake Geneva Playboy Club.

One Sunday afternoon, I was dazzling a group of resort guests with card tricks, magic and sleight of hand illusions. A young lady approached me afterwards and said, *"I have a puzzle for you. Imagine there are three frogs, sitting on a log, floating in the water. If one of the frogs decides to jump off, how many frogs are left?"*

I said there would be two frogs left. She replied, *"No, there are three frogs left."* I didn't get it. She explained, *"Deciding to jump off and actually jumping off are two completely different things."* She was right.

Buried inside that riddle is one of the key principles for conquering change.

You can *decide* to do something.
Or you can *actually do it.*

How much unfinished business do you have? How many things have you *decided* to do but haven't gotten around to doing?

Father time takes no prisoners.

Stop deciding and start doing.

TAKE ACTION! Take your best shot and go for it. Winners are losers who got up and gave it just one more try.

ABOUT THE AUTHOR

Robert Ian is an Author, Hypnotist and Motivational Speaker. His worldwide consulting and publishing firm specializes in personal and organizational change. His break-through book *How To Identify, Master And Conquer Change* helps individuals and organizations uncover the hidden opportunities that surround them at every moment. Robert believes learning should be interactive and fun.  His unique Business Theater™ presentations combine enter-tainment plus a message. Robert has appeared on ABC, CBS, NBC and the FOX television networks. He has delivered over 2000 professional appearances for audiences of 10 to 4000 with clients from Anthem to Zenith. He speaks to corporations, trade associations, government agencies, healthcare organizations, educational institutions, franchises and small businesses.

ORDER FORM
QUANTITY BOOK DISCOUNTS

How To Identify, Master And Conquer Change

An investment in yourself always yields the best return.
Buy one for each member of your organization.

1-9 copies	____	copies at $14.95 each
10-49 copies	____	copies at $13.95 each
50-99 copies	____	copies at $11.95 each
100-249 copies	____	copies at $ 9.95 each
250-499 copies	____	copies at $ 9.50 each
500-999 copies	____	copies at $ 8.95 each
1,000 or more copies	____	copies at $ 8.50 each

Name _____

JobTitle _____

Organization _____

Address _____

City _____ State ____ Zip _____

Phone _____ Fax_____

Email _____

Applicable sales tax, shipping and handling charges will be added to
all quantity book orders. Prices subject to change.

Name on Card _____

Card Number _____ Exp. Date_____

Signature _____ Date_____

Order Online: www.HandbooksForSuccess.com
Fax order to: 608-527-5990
Phone: 800-800-6194
Or mail this form to the address below

Robert Ian Productions, Inc. • PO Box 250 • New Glarus, WI 53574

ORDER FORM
HYPNOSIS MADE EASY™ SELF-HYPNOSIS CDs

Stop Smoking	_____	CDs at $9.95 each
Lose Weight	_____	CDs at $9.95 each
Great Golf	_____	CDs at $9.95 each
Sleep Easy	_____	CDs at $9.95 each
Sales Power	_____	CDs at $9.95 each
Success Habits	_____	CDs at $9.95 each
Breaking Mental Barriers	_____	CDs at $9.95 each
Stress-Free Relaxation	_____	CDs at $9.95 each
EZ Public Speaking	_____	CDs at $9.95 each

For motivational and relaxation purposes only. Use of these CDs promises no health benefits. Individual results may vary.

BOOKS AND LIVE PRESENTATIONS ON CD

How To Identify, Master And Conquer Change on CD *read by the author*
_____ CDs at $14.95 each

The Greatest Secret Never Told *90 minute motivational talk on CD*
_____ CDs at $14.95 each

Name _____

JobTitle _____

Organization _____

Address _____

City _____ State _____ Zip _____

Phone _____ Fax_____

Email _____

A shipping and handling charge of $4.95 will be added to your CD order.
WI residents add 5.5% sales tax. Prices subject to change.

Name on Card _____

Card Number _____ Exp. Date_____

Signature _____ Date_____

Order Online: www.HandbooksForSuccess.com
Fax order to: 608-527-5990
Phone: 800-800-6194
Or mail this form to the address below

Robert Ian Productions, Inc. • PO Box 250 • New Glarus, WI 53574